Firestone B
Success Begins Here

A Christmas Carol
25 Key Quotations for GCSE

Heather Hawkins

Series Editor: Hannah Rabey

firestonebooks.com

A Christmas Carol
25 Key Quotations for GCSE
Heather Hawkins

Series Editor: Hannah Rabey

Text © Heather Hawkins
About this Book section © Hannah Rabey

Cover © XL Book Cover Design
xlbookcoverdesign.co.uk

2021 Edition

ISBN-13: 978-1909608313

Published by Firestone Books

This guide is not endorsed by or affiliated with any exam boards/awarding bodies.

firestonebooks.com

You can stay up to date by following Firestone Books on Facebook and Twitter, or subscribing to our fabulous newsletter.
Go on – you know you want to…

Contents

About this Book

The GCSE English Literature exam relies on understanding a wide range of relevant references, studied both in lessons and as part of revision. This guide will provide you with in-depth analysis of 25 key quotations in Charles Dickens' novella *A Christmas Carol*, written by experts to ensure that you are prepared for success.

In this guide you will find:

- A biography of Charles Dickens' life
- A summary of the key events in each chapter of the novella
- 25 key analysed quotations
- A key terms glossary (key terms are denoted by an asterisk)

The 25 quotations include:

- Detailed analysis of the quotation
- Key context relating to the quotation
- A list of key themes and characters that the quotation links to

A Biography of Charles Dickens

Charles John Huffam Dickens was born in Portsmouth, England on 7 February 1812, the second in a family of eight children. His father, John Dickens, was a clerk in the Navy Pay Office and married Dickens' mother, Elizabeth (née Barrow), in 1809. The family moved to London in 1815 when John was posted there, and later to Sheerness and Chatham, Kent where Dickens attended school.

John and Elizabeth enjoyed entertaining and often held parties and dinners at their home. However, with a large family to support and the costs of their social lifestyle they soon fell into financial difficulty. In the early nineteenth century the failure to pay debts often lead to imprisonment in a debtors' prison. This harsh system was rather counterproductive. Not only was the debtor punished for being in debt, but he or she had little chance of settling the debt because of an inability to earn any wages whilst imprisoned. There was also a social stigma attached to being in debt. In 1824 John Dickens was imprisoned in Marshalsea Debtors' Prison for three months. To assist with the family finances, the young Dickens had to leave school and go out to work. Conditions were harsh and Dickens worked ten hours every day at a blacking (shoe polish) warehouse where his duties involved making paper lids for the blacking pots, tying them with string and sticking a label on the front. Dickens earned a meagre six shillings per week (roughly 30 pence) for this labourious job and you can only imagine how boring and repetitive it must have been! These experiences at the blacking factory are described as told by Dickens to his biographer, John Forster, in *The Life of Charles Dickens* (Boston: James R. Osgood and Company, 1875) vol I, p.52:

"The blacking-warehouse was the last house on the left-hand side of the way, at old Hungerford Stairs. It was a crazy, tumble-down old house, abutting of course on the river, and literally overrun with rats. Its wainscoted rooms, and its rotten floors and staircase, and the old grey rats swarming down in the cellars, and the sound of their squeaking and scuffling coming up the stairs at all times, and the dirt and decay of the place, rise up visibly before me, as if I were there again. The counting-house was on the first floor, looking over the coal-barges and the river. There was a recess in it, in which I was to sit and work. My work was to cover the pots of paste-blacking; first with a piece of oil-paper, and then with a piece of blue paper; to tie them round with a string; and then to clip the paper close and neat, all round, until it looked as smart as a pot of ointment from an apothecary's shop. When a certain number of grosses of pots had attained this pitch of perfection, I was to paste on each a printed label, and then go on again with more pots. Two or three other boys were kept at similar duty down-stairs on similar wages. One of them came up, in a ragged apron and a paper cap, on the first Monday morning, to show me the trick of using the string and tying the knot. His name was Bob Fagin; and I took the liberty of using his name, long afterwards, in Oliver Twist."

Owing to the family's financial situation, Dickens received little formal schooling at this time. His experiences at the blacking factory fuelled an ambition to be educated and increase his career prospects alongside a long-term concern with the plight of the poor, particularly children, in Victorian society. It can be argued that Dickens' early experiences influenced his social consciousness and the content of his novels, such as *David Copperfield, Oliver Twist* and *A Christmas Carol*.

At the age of fourteen, after his father's release from prison, Dickens became a clerk in a solicitor's office. He was an intelligent boy, keen to do well, and studied shorthand to a very high standard, a skill which would stand him in excellent stead as a journalist. In 1829 he began work as a freelance journalist and reported on law cases. Then, in 1831 Dickens became a parliamentary reporter and began writing short stories, the first of which was published in 1833. In 1834 Dickens became a reporter for the *Morning Chronicle* and met Catherine Hogarth, the daughter of the editor. He married Catherine in 1836 and they had ten children. The marriage was not a happy one and Dickens was rumoured to have had an affair. The couple later separated.

From 1836 to his death in 1870 Dickens became established as one of the foremost authors of the Victorian period. Dickens' literary output was prolific. He wrote numerous short stories and fifteen novels. Many have since been adapted for film and television such as *A Christmas Carol, Oliver Twist, Great Expectations* and *David Copperfield* and his works remain in print to this day.

Dickens died following a stroke, possibly brought on by overwork, on 9 June 1870, aged fifty-eight. He was buried at Westminster Abbey.

A Summary of the Key Events in *A Christmas Carol*

As has been seen, Dickens' personal experiences largely influenced the context and thematic concerns of his novels and short stories. *A Christmas Carol* is a novella, a piece of writing of roughly 60 to 120 pages, longer than a short story but considerably shorter than a full-length novel. The novella is divided into five chapters or 'staves', reflecting the theme of a musical carol mentioned in the title of the novella and the musical stave upon which notes are written on sheet music.

The novella was written for publication at Christmas. The Victorians enjoyed Christmas stories and in an era before television, families would spend time reading novellas aloud to each other during the evening for entertainment. These Christmas stories often had a ghost or other supernatural element. When *A Christmas Carol* was first published on 17 December 1843 it was met with immediate and great success, selling over 5,000 copies by Christmas Eve and has never been out of print since.

The plot of *A Christmas Carol* opens with the miserly Ebenezer Scrooge in his office making his clerk, Bob Cratchit, work in the cold with a very meagre fire. Scrooge's nephew, Fred, offers him an invitation to his Christmas party, which Scrooge refuses. Scrooge also will not give a donation to charity collectors who visit his office. Bob finds the courage to ask Scrooge if he can have a day's holiday on Christmas Day, a request which Scrooge is very reluctant to grant. He finally grants it with the condition that Bob starts work earlier on Boxing Day.

Later, Scrooge returns home and is visited by the ghost of his old business partner, Jacob Marley, who warns Scrooge that he will be visited by three spirits. Marley also warns Scrooge to repent of his miserly and mean-spirited ways or he will be destined never to find peace in the afterlife, just as Marley himself has never found peace. The first of the spirits, the Ghost of Christmas Past, visits Scrooge and shows him flashbacks from his lonely childhood, apprenticeship as a clerk and failed engagement to Belle due to his idolisation of money.

The Ghost of Christmas Present then appears and shows Scrooge scenes from the present such as the impoverished Cratchit family's modest but happy Christmas celebrations. Scrooge is saddened by the plight of Tiny Tim, Bob's disabled but kind-natured young son. The Ghost then takes Scrooge to Fred's Christmas party. Although his celebrations are much more lavish than the Cratchits', they are no less happy. Both celebrations highlight the importance of friends and family at Christmas and emphasise Scrooge's self-inflicted social isolation*.

In the fourth stave, or chapter, Scrooge meets the last of the Spirits, the Ghost of Christmas Yet to Come, where he is led by the ghost to the death scene of a man with no one to mourn him. Scrooge is then taken to a graveyard and to a neglected grave with the inscription 'EBENEZER SCROOGE' engraved on the headstone. Filled with horror at his fate, Scrooge sets about mending his ways and becomes the embodiment of Christmas itself. He sends the Cratchits a huge turkey and joins in Fred's Christmas party. Ultimately, Scrooge lives the rest of his days filled with the spirit of Christmas. He increases Bob's salary, improves Bob's poor working conditions and becomes like a second father to Tiny Tim, rendering his redemption complete.

The main themes in *A Christmas Carol* are poverty and social responsibility, family versus isolation, greed and money, Christmas and redemption, all of which will be explored in the key quotations which follow.

A Christmas Carol

25 Key Quotations for GCSE

Stave One

> "Oh! But he was a tight-fisted, hard at the grindstone, Scrooge! A squeezing, wrenching, grasping, scraping, clutching covetous old sinner! Hard and sharp as flint, from which no steel had ever struck out generous fire; secret and self-contained and as solitary as an oyster."

Analysis

The narrator uses figurative language in this quotation to describe Scrooge's unpleasant character. In the first sentence a list of present participles* and adjectives portray to the reader the extent and consistency of Scrooge's greedy and miserly ways. For example, 'Squeezing, wrenching, grasping, scraping, clutching' all suggest that Scrooge literally takes everything he can from everything and everybody. The use of present participles give a sense of this behaviour as ongoing and current and having a negative effect on those surrounding him. The choice of language here indicates Scrooge's obsession with taking all he can, suggesting he is frenzied in his quest to store up more wealth and save money. He is also 'a covetous old sinner!' The verb 'covetous' means to desire to own someone else's property and refers to one of the Biblical Ten Commandments 'Thou shalt not covet thy neighbour's property'. Victorian society was much more inherently religious than society today and the adjective 'covetous' would immediately have had religious connotations for the Victorian reader. This religious context is closely followed and emphasised by 'old sinner' and indicates Scrooge is presented as the antithesis* of Christian values of the time. It is worth noting too that Dickens often gave public readings of his novels and in many ways the texts are written for performance as well as readership. Dickens' use of the list technique in this quotation lends itself to a dramatic performance which emphasises these words for maximum impact.

The second section of the quotation uses a simile* to describe Scrooge's cold personality. Drawing upon imagery from the natural world, Scrooge is described as 'hard and sharp as flint'. Flint is a very hard rock, commonly used to make cutting tools in the Prehistoric Period. Dickens extends the simile by continuing: 'from which no steel had ever struck out generous fire'. This refers to the striking of a piece of steel against flint to create a hot spark and ignite fire. 'No generous fire' emits from Scrooge, however, indicating his cold, stubborn and unyielding character who radiates no vital warmth or compassion towards others. Scrooge is also likened to a 'solitary oyster'. As oyster shells are notoriously difficult to open this simile suggests that Scrooge shuts himself off from society with no desire for friendship or human contact other than the services others may provide for him in order to increase his wealth.

Key Characters

Scrooge

Key Themes

Greed
Isolation
Money

Quotation 2

Stave One

"The cold within him froze his old features, nipped his pointed nose, shrivelled his cheek, stiffened his gait; made his eyes red, his thin lips blue; and spoke out shrewdly in his grating voice. A frosty rime was on his head, and on his eyebrows, and his wiry chin. He carried his own low temperature always about with him; he iced his office in the dog-days; and didn't thaw it one degree at Christmas."

Analysis

In this quotation, written in the narrator's voice, wintry weather is used to describe Scrooge and portray his hard-hearted nature. Just as Scrooge is presented as cold and impenetrable as a person, so also is his physical appearance described as sharp, rigid and unfeeling. It is as though any human warmth has been frozen solid within him as the wintry weather has penetrated his soul.

Pathetic fallacy* is used in this wintry presentation of Scrooge. The winter weather imagery indicates Scrooge has been psychologically frozen, just as nature is stiffened and shrivelled by a heavy frost. Scrooge's appearance is presented as sharp, as though frost has 'nipped his pointed nose' and turned his 'eyes red' and made his 'thin lips blue'. Scrooge also possesses a harsh, thin almost glacial voice to match his physical appearance. The pathetic fallacy is extended as the overall frosty image of Scrooge conjures up the image of Jack Frost whose very persona exudes a cold atmosphere. For example, he has a 'frosty rime on his head'. 'Rime' is frost formed on cold objects by the rapid freezing of water vapour in cloud or fog. This suggests that Scrooge is such a cold character that frost forms upon him.

Scrooge's coldness is inherent to him as he 'carries his cold about him' and radiates coldness as he 'iced his office' even during the 'dog days (hottest days) of summer. Unyielding and cold all year round, Scrooge doesn't 'thaw' or unbend his rigid, cold ways even at Christmas.

Key Characters
Scrooge

Key Themes
Christmas
Isolation

Stave One

"What's Christmas time to you but a time for paying bills without money; a time for finding yourself a year older, and not an hour richer; a time for balancing your books […] every idiot who goes about with 'Merry Christmas,' on his lips, should be boiled with his own pudding, and buried with a stake of holly through his heart."

Analysis

Scrooge's speech is in reaction to his nephew Fred's cheerful Christmas greetings. Scrooge's response suggests his cynical* view of Christmas as just a time to settle unpaid debts in a spirit of good will, whilst not making any profit due to the holiday period. He measures time and the progression of his life in terms of how much richer he becomes hour by hour. Scrooge's view contrasts with Fred's generosity and his willingness to give to charity compared to Scrooge's sharp dismissal of the charity collectors who come to his door.

Scrooge continues with a darkly humorous and hyperbolic assertion of what should happen to those who celebrate Christmas. Bearing in mind that Christmas became increasingly popular during the 1800s, Scrooge's tirade is even more humorous and suggests that the majority of the population should be 'boiled with his own pudding'!

The use of semi-colons and commas emphasise the long, ranting spiel and hyperbole of Scrooge's tirade and its humour, which juxtaposes* the joy of Christmas with violent imagery of the 'stake of holly' through the heart of any person who celebrates it.

Key Characters

Scrooge

Key Themes

Christmas
Greed
Money

Quotation 4

Stave One

"Are there no prisons?" asked Scrooge.

"Plenty of prisons," said the gentleman, laying down the pen again.

"And the Union workhouses?" demanded Scrooge. "Are they still in operation?"

"They are. Still," returned the gentleman," I wish I could say they were not."

"The Treadmill and the Poor Law are in full vigour, then?" said Scrooge.

"Both very busy, sir."

"Oh! I was afraid, from what you said at first, that something had occurred to stop them in their useful course," said Scrooge. "I'm very glad to hear it."

Analysis

The above dialogue occurs between Scrooge and a charity collector who visits his counting house* asking for donations for the poor. Scrooge's response reveals the harsh treatment of the poor in Victorian England. Those who were completely destitute* had no option but to go to the workhouse. Towns and some villages had workhouses and conditions inside were renowned for being very harsh. Husbands, wives and children were separated from each other and had to undertake repetitive and menial tasks such as stone breaking for road laying, wood chopping, rope making and domestic duties. In return, inmates of the workhouse received extremely plain, meagre rations of food and shelter in large dormitories with very primitive conditions.

Scrooge suggests that those who are unable to contribute to the economy, such as the unemployed, the disabled, elderly, orphans and unmarried mothers, should be institutionalised in workhouses and made to pay for their misfortunes. He does not consider that inmates of workhouses or prisons should have any rights or comforts. Scrooge has no conscience about the conditions such people live in and can turn a blind eye to their plight by assuming that state institutions rather than private individuals take responsibility for those on the fringes of society. This rather arrogant point of view is formed from the privilege of the middle-class who were secure in their own economic position. In assuming that the impoverished were conveniently hidden away in state institutions like workhouses, Scrooge deliberately ignores the visible poverty surrounding him on the London streets and his own employee, Bob Cratchit. Scrooge's view of social responsibility is to pass the problem onto the state rather than see how he can use his own wealthy position to help those in need.

Key Characters
Scrooge

Key Themes
Poverty
Social responsibility

Quotation 5

Stave One

"You'll want all day to-morrow, I suppose?" said Scrooge.

"If quite convenient, sir."

"It's not convenient," said Scrooge, "and it's not fair. If I was to stop half-a-crown for it, you'd think yourself ill-used, I'll be bound?" […] "And yet," said Scrooge, "you don't think *me* ill-used, when I pay a day's wages for no work."

Analysis

This dialogue takes place between Scrooge and his clerk, Bob Cratchit when Bob asks Scrooge's permission to have a day's holiday on Christmas Day.

This quotation is relevant to the themes of social responsibility and poverty in the novella as working-class people had very few employment rights in Victorian England. Wages were often kept as low as possible, there was no sick pay or official holidays (paid or unpaid). Employees could be sacked for any minor mishap and have no right or opportunity to appeal. A sacked employee would have great difficulty in finding another job. It would not have been an automatic right for Bob to be given a day's holiday on Christmas Day and he shows great courage in asking for the day off. This indicates how important family life is for Bob and highlights the lack of basic rights for the working-class which we now take for granted.

In granting Bob's holiday Scrooge considers himself to be 'ill-used' by Bob and likens it to 'picking a man's pocket', implying that he is the victim of theft. This hyperbolic reaction equates the rights of employees with criminal activity and suggests Scrooge accepts no social responsibility for working conditions and the low salary of his employee. In a period when trade unions* were illegal until 1871, Scrooge's view does not seem too unusual. Against this pro-employer's stance, however, was a growing band of social reformers such as Charles Dickens, Elizabeth Gaskill, William Booth and Lord Shaftesbury who brought social injustice to the notice of the public and campaigned for social reform.

Key Characters
Bob Cratchit
Scrooge

Key Themes
Poverty
Social responsibility

Quotation 6

Stave One

"Scrooge took the melancholy dinner in his usual melancholy tavern; and having read all the newspapers, and beguiled the rest of the evening with his banker's-book, went home to bed."

Analysis

This quotation occurs in Stave One following the closure of Scrooge's office late on Christmas Eve.

Scrooge takes his 'melancholy dinner' alone in a 'melancholy tavern' indicating that even his mealtimes are as dreary as Scrooge is himself. The repetition of 'melancholy' suggests that Scrooge purposely chooses a dingy tavern to eat in as it suits his temperament. The meal is 'melancholy' and lonely without company.

In contrast to Bob and Fred, Scrooge has no family or friends to go home to. His only companions are newspapers and his banker's book, making money his closest relation and the root of his isolation.

The use of semi-colons and commas in this quotation creates a sense of the progression of time during Scrooge's evening routine, but also emphasises the relentless dreariness of Scrooge's life and his continuous self-inflicted social isolation.

Key Characters

Scrooge

Key Themes

Isolation versus family

Money

Quotation 7

Stave Two

"He then made bold to inquire what business brought him there.

'Your welfare!' said the Ghost.

Scrooge expressed himself much obliged, but could not help thinking that a night of unbroken rest would have been conducive to that end. The Spirit must have heard him thinking for it said immediately:

'Your reclamation, then. Take heed!'"

Analysis

Redemption is a key theme in this quotation.

The Ghost of Christmas Past asserts that he is concerned with Scrooge's 'welfare', which Scrooge humorously misinterprets to mean the physical comfort of a good night's sleep. The welfare of mortals, in the Ghost's opinion, is more concerned with the spiritual well-being of humans.

In Victorian society, where religion was deeply entrenched in everyday life, the Christian belief in heaven and hell was very profound. Redemption for one's sins was considered the key to entry into heaven after death.

The ghost offers Scrooge the opportunity of redemption to enable him to go to heaven in the afterlife.

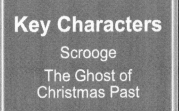

Key Characters

Scrooge

The Ghost of
Christmas Past

Key Themes

Redemption

Quotation 8

Stave Two

"I wish," Scrooge muttered, putting his hand in his pocket, and looking about him, after drying his eyes with his cuff: "but it's too late now."

"What is the matter?" asked the Spirit.

"Nothing," said Scrooge. "Nothing. There was a boy singing a Christmas Carol at my door last night. I should like to have given him something: that's all."

Analysis

Scrooge's spoken thoughts in this quotation signify the beginning of his redemption. Scrooge starts to consider the effects of his own behaviour upon others and acknowledges that he should have acted differently and could still do so.

Redemption can be defined as the saving of a person from evil or suffering. The purpose of the three spirits in *A Christmas Carol* is to show Scrooge the error of his ways and save himself from going to hell in the afterlife. Religious belief was very deeply entrenched in Victorian society, with a firm belief in God and the afterlife. Those who had lived a good, kind life, it was believed, would be rewarded with eternal life in heaven, whilst those who lived unkindly and selfishly would go to hell. Hell was perceived as a place of intense suffering and was often imagined to be a pit of fire. Redemption was considered a possibility providing an individual saw the error of their ways and changed their outlook on life and their behaviour. As such, *A Christmas Carol* is a cautionary and moral tale of what can happen if an individual is willing to be saved from hell through the opportunity for redemption.

Key Characters

Scrooge

The Ghost of Christmas Past

Key Themes

Redemption

Quotation 9

Stave Two

"He has spent but a few pounds of your mortal money: three or four, perhaps. Is that so much that he deserves this praise?"

"It isn't that," said Scrooge, heated by the remark, and speaking unconsciously like his former, not his latter, self. "It isn't that, Spirit. He has the power to render us happy or unhappy; to make our service light or burdensome; a pleasure or a toil. Say that his power lies in words and looks; in things so slight and insignificant that it is impossible to add and count 'em up; what then? The happiness he gives, is quite as great as if it cost a fortune."

Analysis

Scrooge makes this observation when the first Spirit takes Scrooge back in time to when he was a young apprentice and his employer, Mr Fezziwig, throws a modest Christmas party for his employees with music, dancing and food. Scrooge acknowledges the positive and negative effects an employer can have upon the workforce and that the way in which a day's work can be pleasurable or arduous is largely down to the attitude of the employer. Scrooge remembers the happiness Fezziwig generated by his kind generosity and realises that it is worth as much as if he had spent a fortune.

It is notable that Scrooge 'speaks unconsciously like his former, not his latter, self'. This suggests that Scrooge did not begin his adult life with such a mercenary mindset and that his idolisation of money has slowly taken hold of him over the years. The fact that he speaks 'unconsciously' suggests the Spirit is starting to probe and reveal the original Scrooge, before a Capitalist love of money took hold of him. This acknowledgement by Scrooge suggests he is starting to remember again that qualities such as happiness and generosity far outweigh monetary value. This is furthered as Scrooge wishes he could speak to Bob Cratchit, and in the final stave when Scrooge finally accepts social responsibility and acts upon it by increasing Bob's salary.

Key Characters

Scrooge

Key Themes

Poverty
Social responsibility

Quotation 10

Stave Two

"It matters little," she said, softly. "To you, very little. Another idol displaced me; and if it can cheer and comfort you in time to come, as I would have tried to do, I have no just cause to grieve."

"What Idol has displaced you?" he rejoined.

"A golden one."

Analysis

This quotation occurs when the Ghost of Christmas Past takes Scrooge back to the time when his fiancée, Belle, breaks off their engagement because money has become more important to Scrooge than their relationship. Belle suggests to Scrooge that money has become his 'idol', indicating that he worships money as a god. Scrooge retaliates by arguing that poverty is the hard reality of the world and that wealth is the route out of poverty.

This quotation demonstrates that Scrooge's greed and idolisation of money costs him in terms of human relationships which far outweigh material wealth. This is furthered in Stave Four following Scrooge's death when no one mourns him. Even his possessions are sold to a second-hand shop for as much profit as can be made, indicating that Scrooge has died as he has lived by reducing the value of human life to material wealth.

His fear of poverty is understandable, though, given the immense poverty suffered across Victorian Britain. However, Scrooge takes his quest to avoid poverty too far and becomes obsessed with making and saving money. In doing so, he exacerbates poverty as he takes wealth rather than using his money to help those less fortunate than himself.

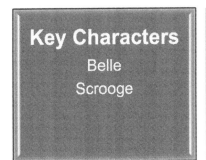

Key Characters
Belle
Scrooge

Key Themes
Family
Greed
Money
Social responsibility

Quotation 11

Stave Two

"His partner lies upon the point of death, I hear; and there he sat alone. Quite alone in the world, I do believe."

Analysis

This dialogue is spoken by Belle's (Scrooge's ex-fiancée) husband, as Jacob Marley, Scrooge's business partner, is dying. Once Marley dies, the dialogue suggests, Scrooge will be entirely alone as Marley, a business associate, is the closest he has to a friend. It is notable that their relationship is based upon and cemented by money and greed rather than affection and friendship. It follows the appearance of Marley's ghost to Scrooge in Stave One when Marley advises him to change his ways or he will suffer the same fate of no peace in the afterlife.

Key Characters
Belle's husband
Scrooge

Key Themes
Greed
Money
Family versus isolation

Quotation 12

Stave Three

"In came little Bob, the father, with at least three feet of comforter exclusive of the fringe, hanging down before him; and his thread-bare clothes darned up and brushed, to look seasonable; and Tiny Tim, he bore a little crutch, and had his limbs supported by an iron frame!"

Analysis

The above quotation, written in the narrator's voice, occurs when Bob Cratchit returns home late on Christmas Eve from his job as a clerk in Scrooge's office, having been begrudgingly granted Christmas Day off by Scrooge. Although Scrooge is the epitome of the hard-hearted employer, the average working-class employee had very few employment rights in the Victorian period and time off would have been considered a luxury which many employers were reluctant to grant. The minimal employment laws protecting the rights of workers meant low pay, and poor and dangerous working conditions. Furthermore, non-existent health and safety were the norm for the majority of the working-class population, and many employees suffered accidents and even death at work due to dangerous machinery and conditions.

The poverty in which most families lived is evident in this description of Bob wearing only a 'comforter' (a scarf) as he has no coat and only threadbare clothes. The narrator uses quite a patronising tone when describing Bob as 'little', though this could indicate his small stature because he is malnourished. The adjective 'little' also evokes more reader sympathy, as it prompts an image of a small man struggling to survive and provide for his family against the might of Scrooge and the Capitalism* he represents.

We are given the impression, however, that Bob and his wife are proud people who do their utmost to maintain a respectable standard of living. Bob's clothes are 'darned up and brushed to look seasonable', indicating his pride in his appearance despite his poverty and his determination to celebrate Christmas, despite his daily struggles. Bob's determination to spend Christmas Day with his family confirms him to be a devoted husband and father as is his carrying of his young disabled son, Tiny Tim, on his shoulders.

Key Characters
Bob Cratchit
Tiny Tim

Key Themes
Family
Poverty

Quotation 13

Stave Three

Bob says of his disabled son, Tiny Tim:

"As good as gold," said Bob, "and better. Somehow he gets thoughtful sitting by himself so much, and thinks the strangest things you ever heard. He told me, coming home, that he hoped the people saw him in church, because he was a cripple, and it might be pleasant to them to remember upon Christmas Day, who made lame beggars walk and blind men see."

Analysis

The above quotation, with its reference to the New Testament accounts of Jesus healing the sick, suggests that Tiny Tim is a deep-thinking and pious* child. Dickens often included a disadvantaged child character in his novels to highlight more clearly the social comment he wished to make. Such a child character increases the pathos* in the narrative* and helps to invoke reader empathy* for his social message. Tiny Tim is doubly disadvantaged both as the son of poverty-stricken parents and as a child with disabilities. Such children were extremely vulnerable in mid-Victorian England due to the lack of education for the working-classes and their unsuitability for work due to their disability, making their long-term prospects bleak.

Tiny Tim is relatively fortunate as he has a loving and supportive family even though they struggle economically. In real life many disabled children were far less fortunate and would have had no choice but to live in a workhouse. The life expectancy of a Victorian disabled child would have been much less than today. This was due to malnutrition and lack of affordable and effective healthcare as there was no National Health Service and patients had to pay to see a doctor. Although these factors impacted upon every working-class person, a child with disabilities would have faced additional challenges to their health. Such vulnerability is reiterated by Tiny Tim's death in Stave Four.

Tiny Tim's piety, thoughtfulness and his ability to see the good in a bleak situation contrasts sharply with Scrooge's inhumane and uncharitable outlook and behaviour. As such, Tiny Tim becomes instrumental in Scrooge's redemption as it is largely through his concern for Tiny Tim that he starts to see the error of his ways.

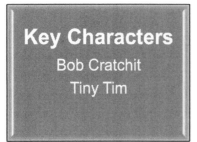

Key Characters
Bob Cratchit
Tiny Tim

Key Themes
Poverty
Redemption
Religion

Quotation 14

Stave Three

"There never was such a goose. [...] Its tenderness and flavour, size and cheapness, were themes of universal admiration. Eked out by the apple-sauce and mashed potatoes, it was a sufficient dinner for the whole family; indeed, as Mrs Cratchit said with great delight (surveying one small atom of a bone upon the dish), they hadn't ate it all at last!"

Analysis

This quotation forms part of a lengthy description of the Cratchits' Christmas celebrations during which their dinner is described in minute detail.

Goose was a very popular choice for a Victorian Christmas dinner, much in the same way as many families choose turkey for Christmas dinner today. The small size of the Cratchits' goose is expressed along with its cheapness. The family have bought the biggest goose they can afford but each of them has only a woefully small portion which needs to be 'eked out' by mashed potatoes and apple sauce. This is reiterated when Mrs Cratchit notices a small piece of bone left on the dish suggesting that goose is a rare treat and the family have literally eaten every morsel. It is noticeable that the only accompaniments to the goose are mashed potatoes and apple sauce. There are no other vegetables on the table, suggesting the purchase of the goose has taken most of the family's budget for their Christmas dinner.

The effort which went into the preparation of the Cratchits' dinner and their great appreciation of it suggests the importance the family attach to Christmas celebrations, despite their poverty. Sometimes working-class families would pay into a 'goose club' run by their local butcher to spread the cost of their Christmas goose, but in doing so they have suffered greater hardship as there was less available money for food and heating on a day-to-day basis throughout the year. This willingness to suffer increased hardship suggests the importance the Victorians attributed to celebrating Christmas and observing its traditions.

Key Characters
The Cratchit family

Key Themes
Christmas
Poverty

Quotation 15

Stave Three

"Then all the Cratchit family drew round the hearth, [...] and at Bob Cratchit's elbow stood the family display of glass; two tumblers, and a custard-cup without a handle.

These held the hot stuff from the jug, however, as well as golden goblets would have done; Bob served it out with beaming looks, while the chestnuts on the fire sputtered and crackled noisily. Then Bob proposed:

'Merry Christmas to us all, my dears. God Bless us!'

Which all the family re-echoed.

'God bless us every one!' said Tiny Tim, the last of all."

Analysis

The closeness of the Cratchit family is emphasised in this quotation, which forms part of a detailed description of their Christmas celebrations in Stave Three. The narrator draws attention to the 'semi-circle' which the family form when gathering around their fireplace together, which illustrates their closeness and willingness to share the small amount of heat and light they can afford.

The meagre collection of glassware from which the family drink a cheap alcoholic beverage of gin and lemons is grandly named 'the family display of glass', suggesting they cherish it as much as if it were a priceless family heirloom and forms part of the collective family wealth. This is reiterated by the reference to 'golden goblets'.

The overall mood of the scene is one of contentment and equality within the Cratchit family relationships. Bob shares out the drink equally 'with beaming looks' and ensures everyone has a taste. Even the chestnuts roasting on the fire join in the genial conversation as they 'sputtered and crackled noisily'. Bob raises a toast to his family, wishing all of them a Merry Christmas, which is echoed by the family, especially by Tiny Tim.

This quotation contrasts strongly with the image of Scrooge spending Christmas Eve with only his bank book for company and emphasises the importance of family to the Victorians, especially at Christmas.

Key Characters

Bob Cratchit
The Cratchit family
Tiny Tim

Key Themes

Christmas
Poverty
Family versus isolation

Quotation 16

Stave Three

"Spirit," said Scrooge, with an interest he had never felt before, "tell me if Tiny Tim will live."

"I see a vacant seat," replied the Ghost, "[...] If these shadows remain unaltered by the Future, the child will die."

"No, no," said Scrooge. "Oh no kind Spirit! say he will be spared."

"If these shadows remain unaltered by the Future, none other of my race," returned the Ghost, "will find him here. What then? If he be like to die, he had better do it, and decrease the surplus population."

Scrooge hung his head to hear his own words quoted by the Spirit, and was overcome with penitence* and grief.

Analysis

Scrooge's redemption* begins with his concern for Tiny Tim. In this quotation Scrooge manages to show some compassion for Tiny Tim's plight and for the grieving Cratchit family, and pleads with the Spirit to tell him that Tiny Tim will be spared. In response the Spirit proposes that unless the 'shadows' blotting society are removed then Tiny Tim will die. The Spirit quotes Scrooge's own previous words against him: 'If he be like to die, he had better do it, and decrease the surplus population.'

Many people viewed poverty in Victorian England as a consequence of a rapidly growing population, especially in the cities, as urbanisation increased dramatically due to the Industrial Revolution. Scrooge is ashamed of his view and is overcome with remorse, which is a huge step towards his redemption and eventual improvement of his ways.

Key Characters

Scrooge

The Ghost of Christmas Present

Key Themes

Poverty

Redemption

Quotation 17

Stave Three

"Mr Scrooge!" said Bob, "I'll give you Mr Scrooge, the Founder of the Feast!"

"The Founder of the Feast indeed!" cried Mrs Cratchit, reddening. "I wish I had him here. I'd give him a piece of my mind to feast upon, and I hope he'd have a good appetite for it."

"My dear," said Bob, "the children; Christmas Day."

"It should be Christmas Day, I am sure," said she, "on which one drinks the health of such an odious, stingy, hard, unfeeling man as Mr Scrooge. You know he is, Robert! Nobody knows it better than you do, poor fellow!"

"My dear," was Bob's mild answer, "Christmas Day."

Analysis

The above exchange between Bob Cratchit and his wife takes place after the Cratchit family have enjoyed their meagre Christmas dinner just as much as if it had been a huge banquet. They are delighted to all be together on Christmas Day suggesting they are a close-knit family. Bob's eldest children have also been granted a holiday on Christmas Day enabling the whole family to celebrate together. It is for these reasons that Bob proposes a toast to Scrooge and in doing so demonstrates his humility in acknowledging he is at the mercy of his employer. Bob possesses great generosity of spirit in his unwillingness to criticise Scrooge. Bob's gentle, passive nature is emphasised when the narrator describes Bob's reaction to Mrs Cratchit's realistic opinion of Scrooge as 'mild'. This doesn't suggest that Bob disagrees with his wife but that he doesn't want to mar the few precious hours the family have together to enjoy Christmas with negative feelings.

Although Bob may not outwardly rebel against his employer and the impoverished conditions he, his family and the working-class at large are forced to endure, he is astute and acutely aware that if he asks for a rise in his salary and improvement in working conditions he could easily be sacked. This would place his family in a worse financial position and nearer to having to succumb to living at the workhouse.

This quotation demonstrates that Bob is kind, generous and passive, but it also indicates an understanding that his economic situation could actually be far worse and values the precious joy he shares with his family. Bob is dedicated enough to endure considerable hardship to give his family as good a standard of living as his class* position allows.

Key Characters

Bob Cratchit

Mrs Cratchit

Key Themes

Christmas

Poverty

Family versus isolation

Quotation 18

Stave Three

"They were not a handsome family; they were not well dressed; their shoes were far from being water-proof; their clothes were scanty; and Peter might have known, and very likely did, the inside of a pawn-broker's. But they were happy, grateful, pleased with one another, and contented with the time."

Analysis

In this quotation, which forms part of a lengthy description of the Cratchit family's Christmas celebrations in Stave Three, the poverty that the Cratchit family suffer is also emphasised.

The narrator draws attention to their lack of adequate clothing. The clothing they do have is threadbare and they are wearing old, well-worn shoes. Peter, Bob's eldest son, the quotation suggests, may be familiar with the pawnbroker's shop. A pawnbroker was a shop where people who needed money urgently could exchange property such as jewellery or household goods in return for a loan of money, then reclaim their property when they could afford to re-pay the loan. Pawning property was a source of income for poor families, especially during times of additional hardship. Overriding this poverty, however, is the happiness of the Cratchit family and the gratitude* for the things they do have.

The closeness of the Cratchit family is emphasised by a list of positive adjectives: 'happy, grateful, pleased with one another, and contented with the time,' and contrasts sharply with Scrooge's isolation.

Key Characters

The Cratchit family

Key Themes

Christmas

Family versus isolation

Quotation 19

Stave Three

"Blessings on it, how the Ghost exulted! How it bared its breadth of breast, and opened its capacious palm, and floated on, outpouring, with a generous hand, its bright and harmless mirth on everything within its reach!"

Analysis

The above quotation follows a descriptive passage where Scrooge and the Ghost of Christmas Present observe Christmas festivities amongst all classes of Victorian society. The Ghost of Christmas Present personifies* Christmas spirit and this quotation suggests that he spreads his magic across all sectors of society, all of which embrace the Spirit of Christmas, excepting Scrooge. This furthers Scrooge's isolation from society and highlights his mean-spirited ways.

Key Characters
The Ghost of Christmas Present

Key Themes
Family versus isolation
Christmas

Quotation 20

Stave Three

"two men who watched the light had made a fire, that through the loophole in the thick stone wall shed out a ray of brightness on the awful sea. Joining their horny hands over the rough table at which they sat, they wished each other Merry Christmas in their can of grog; and one of them [...] struck up a sturdy song that was like a Gale in itself."

Analysis

This quotation forms part of a wider descriptive section of the narrative during which the Ghost of Christmas Present takes Scrooge on a tour of the United Kingdom to show him how the spirit of Christmas touches and warms the whole nation.

This quotation portrays two lighthouse keepers during a gale, who despite the treacherous conditions at sea and their isolated position in the offshore lighthouse, still find time to celebrate Christmas with a spirit of goodwill towards each other. They enjoy sharing a drink of grog and singing together.

Once more Dickens emphasises the universal joy of Christmas to illustrate the contrast between the goodwill of the lighthouse keepers and the miserly, miserable Scrooge more clearly.

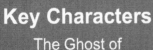

Key Characters

The Ghost of Christmas Present

Key Themes

Family versus isolation

Christmas

Quotation 21

Stave Three

"I am sorry for him; I couldn't be angry with him if I tried. Who suffers by his ill whims! Himself, always. Here, he takes it into his head to dislike us, and he won't come and dine with us. What's the consequence? He don't lose much of a dinner."

Analysis

This speech, given by Fred, Scrooge's nephew, demonstrates Fred's kind and generous nature.

Fred is the antithesis of Scrooge as he is charitable to everyone. He willingly gives to the poor and even invites the miserable Scrooge for Christmas dinner.

Fred personifies all that the Victorians considered to be Christian values, especially at Christmas time: charity and social responsibility, and the importance of goodwill and family life.

In this quotation Fred demonstrates this kind and generous spirit by expressing his sympathy for Scrooge and suggests that Scrooge ultimately loses out through his disengagement with others and his refusal to join in the Christmas festivities. Scrooge does not need to isolate himself in this way, but choses to do so.

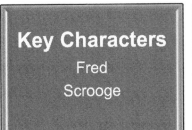

Key Characters

Fred

Scrooge

Key Themes

Christmas

Family versus isolation

Quotation 22

Stave Three

"But they didn't devote the whole evening to music. After a time they played at forfeits; for it is good to be children sometimes, and never better than at Christmas, when its mighty Founder was a child Himself. Stop! There was first a game of blind-man's buff. Of course there was."

Analysis

The above quotation forms part of a detailed description of Fred's Christmas celebrations and portrays the types of entertainment the Victorians enjoyed at Christmas. Before the age of radio and television, the Victorians had to make their own entertainment and enjoyed music, dance and party games. Even adults joined in with games which are now considered children's games.

As can be seen from this description, the middle-class was no less enthusiastic about Christmas than the working-class and indicates Christmas was very important to all sectors of society.

This quotation explicitly links Christmas to Christianity and the birth of Christ by reference to Jesus, the 'mighty Founder' of the festivities. Central to Christmas was a profound belief in God and the Christmas story. Scrooge's rejection of Christmas ultimately rejects Christianity and the moral values the Victorians associated with a belief in God.

Key Characters

Narrator

Key Themes

Christmas

Quotation 23

Stave Three

"From the foldings of its robe, it brought two children; wretched, abject, frightful, hideous, miserable. [...] They were a boy and a girl. Yellow, meagre, ragged, scowling, wolfish, but prostrate, too, in their humility. Where graceful youth should have filled their features out, and touched them with its freshest tints, a stale and shrivelled hand, like that of age, had pinched, and twisted them, and pulled them into shreds [...]

"Spirit! Are they yours?" Scrooge could say no more.

"They are Man's," said the Spirit, looking down upon them. "And they cling to me, appealing from their fathers. This boy is Ignorance. This girl is Want."

Analysis

This quotation occurs at the end of Stave Three when the Ghost of Christmas Present reveals to Scrooge two impoverished children hidden in the folds of his robe. These two children, who are named 'Ignorance and Want', personify poverty and destitution. Neither child is described in child-like terms. Rather, they are described as though they are not human but mythical beings, phantoms or ghosts – 'wretched', 'frightful', 'hideous'. The children kneel down at the ghost's feet, emphasising their fear and also their lowly status in society.

Their physical appearance suggests they are near to death. They are 'yellow, meagre, ragged, scowling and wolfish'. These children are not rosy-cheeked and healthy as one would expect, instead the yellow tinge to their skin suggests disease. They are also 'meagre' and 'ragged', indicating that they are malnourished, and their clothes are hanging from them in shreds, not adequate to keep them warm.

The expressions of the children are 'scowling and wolfish' as though they have an offensive, animalistic attitude towards society and a savage need to survive and take all they can from others in a vain attempt to satisfy their ravaging hunger. Such children were often considered the 'undeserving poor' by the authorities as they resorted to petty criminal behaviour such as theft of food from market stalls just to eat. These children contrast with the 'respectable' poverty of the Cratchits who, despite their hardship, live within the law. The Cratchit children are fortunate though, as they have supportive parents. For orphans on the streets, particularly in the big cities, a life of hunger, destitution and exploitation* at the hands of adults was as much as they could expect.

The children are also presented as elderly before their years, almost ghost-like and nearing death. Their hands are 'shrivelled' and age has 'pinched and twisted them and pulled them into shreds'. These vivid and violent verbs indicate that poverty has physically deformed the children and has literally wrung childhood out of them. In doing so, they have lost all childhood innocence and are overburdened with far greater concerns, such as the daily struggle to find food, shelter and clothing, than to be able to play.

They can be viewed as an extended metaphor* for the ills of Victorian society and the stark division between those who had nothing and those who had plenty. In portraying the children as prematurely aged, Dickens suggests that poverty prevents Victorian society from fully flourishing and the opposite of a vigorous, healthy society is an ailing social structure which could lead to the demise of the nation.

The Spirit continues to explain to Scrooge that such children belong to us all as everyone has a responsibility to resolve the underlying problems causing such immense poverty. 'They are Man's,' he explains, proposing that as mankind has created such children then the responsibility of relieving their intense suffering rests on us all.

Key Characters	Key Themes
Scrooge The Ghost of Christmas Present	Poverty Social responsibility

Stave Four

"It was shrouded in a deep black garment, which concealed its head, its face, its form, and left nothing of it visible save one outstretched hand. But for this it would have been difficult to detach its figure from the night, and separate it from the darkness by which it was surrounded."

Analysis

The above quotation, in the voice of the narrator, draws upon the Victorian tradition of a Christmas ghost story and its gothic predecessors, during which the fear of the supernatural* was sensationalised. Dickens emphasises the ghost story tradition in his brief Preface to the novel. He asserts:

"I have endeavoured in this Ghostly little book, to raise the Ghost of an Idea, which shall not put my readers out of humour with themselves, with each other, with the season, or with me. May it haunt their house pleasantly, and no one wish to lay it."

'The Ghost of an Idea' suggests Dickens uses a popular genre – the ghost story – to then increase awareness of the main theme of the novella – poverty and social responsibility. In choosing a popular genre to convey his broader, deeper message Dickens ensures he has as large a readership as possible. For the middle-classes, who had the money to spend on Christmas publications, reading a novella aloud was a popular form of entertainment especially during the Christmas period. The novella is short enough to allow time for a complete reading of the volume and ensures Scrooge's social commentary will be completely heard.

The Ghost of Christmas Yet to Come is characterised by an emphasis upon its sense of nothingness as though it is a frightening, indistinct void which fuses with the night sky. This sense of nothingness foreshadows Scrooge's fate if he refuses to repent of his ways as no one will remember him or mourn him when he dies, rendering his life an obsolete void. The obliteration of any memory of Scrooge is dramatised later in Stave Four when the Ghost of Christmas Yet to Come takes Scrooge to a neglected grave and he discovers that this grave is his own. No one has cared to tend to the grave, indicating Scrooge is being shown the same neglect and disregard he meted out to others during his lifetime. Scrooge is as isolated in death as he was in life. No one remembers him or mourns him because of his miserly and cruel ways.

Key Characters

Scrooge

The Ghost of
Christmas Yet to Come

Key Themes

Family versus
isolation

Quotation 25

Stave Four

"Spirit!" he cried, tight clutching at its robe, "hear me! I am not the man I was. I will not be the man I must have been for this intercourse. Why show me this, if I am past all hope?"

[...] "Good Spirit," he pursued, as down upon the ground he fell before it: "Your nature intercedes for me, and pities me. Assure me that I yet may change these shadows you have shown me, by an altered life!"

Analysis

In this quotation, Scrooge acknowledges that the spirits have given him the chance of redemption and the opportunity to change his ways. Scrooge's assertion that the Ghost 'intercedes' for him suggests that the ghost is a mediator between mankind and God. Scrooge is being given the chance to avoid going to hell after his death and to have the chance to change the 'shadows' in his life. These 'shadows' are a metaphor* to describe the hardship and suffering Scrooge has caused through his own greed. A shadow can have a negative, sinister and frightening connotation suggesting that they lurk everywhere Scrooge has been and terrify those he has held power over, such as the Cratchit family. In comparison to Bob Cratchit, who radiates 'beaming looks', Scrooge spreads darkness rather than light. He has the chance to reverse this through the redemption offered to him by all three ghosts.

The novella does end with a little uncertainty as to how genuine Scrooge's redemption is or whether it derives from a fear of punishment in the afterlife. Scrooge's dramatic alteration from miser* to a man with an almost excessive, over-the-top generosity in the closing pages of the novella does support this more cynical view. Alternatively, the Victorians did enjoy a positive resolution to a story and as *A Christmas Carol* was written for Christmas entertainment it would have been seen rather Scrooge-like not to have a happy ending. Ultimately, does Dickens leave it to allow the reader to decide?

Key Characters

Scrooge

The Ghost of
Christmas Yet to Come

Key Themes

Redemption

Glossary of Key Terms

Antithesis: the opposite of something or someone.

Capitalism: an economy that is based on individual people or companies owning and transporting products and services, rather than being owned by the government.

Class: a social structure in Britain, generally considered to be divided into working-class, middle-class and upper-class groups of people.

Counting house: an office where the financial books of businesses are kept.

Cynical: a belief that people are generally dishonest and selfish. To believe the worst of people.

Destitute: to be extremely poor.

Empathy: to understand and share another's experiences and emotions.

Exploitation: to use someone unfairly.

Extended metaphor: a metaphor that continues throughout a section of text.

Gratitude: to feel thankful.

Isolation: to be separate from others.

Juxtapose: to place different things together in order to show that they are similar or different.

Metaphor: to refer to one thing as another thing in order to suggest the two things are similar.

Miser: a person who hoards money and spends very little of it.

Narrative: the plot and story that is told.

Pathetic fallacy: the use of the weather to create a particular tone.

Pathos: to cause people to feel sympathy and sadness, particularly through emotive language or examples.

Penitence: to feel regret or sadness because of something one has done wrong.

Personification: to use human attributes to describe something non-human.

Pious: very religious.

Present participle: a form of a verb that ends in *-ing* and comes after another verb to show continuous action.

Redemption: in Christianity, the act of saving people from sin and evil.

Remorse: to feel sorry or guilty for doing something wrong.

Simile: to compare two things using *like* or *as*.

Supernatural: things that cannot be explained by science or the laws of nature.

Trade union: an association of workers in a particular occupation that is designed to protect pay, working conditions and wellbeing.

Our fabulous new revision guides are out now!

25 Key Quotations for GCSE

- Romeo and Juliet
- A Christmas Carol
- Macbeth
- Dr Jekyll and Mr Hyde
- An Inspector Calls

GCSE Revision Guides

- Dr Jekyll and Mr Hyde
- A Christmas Carol
- Macbeth
- English Language

But that's not all! We've also got a host of annotation-friendly editions, containing oodles of space for you to fill with those all-important notes:

Annotation-Friendly Editions

- Dr Jekyll and Mr Hyde
- A Christmas Carol
- Romeo and Juliet
- Macbeth

… and lots more!

Available through Amazon, Waterstones, and all good bookshops!

About the author of this guide

Heather Hawkins is an English tutor and examiner for Cambridge, tutoring GCSE and A Level syllabi. She is also a director of The Thomas Hardy Association, based at the University of St Andrews. Heather has an ongoing research interest in Victorian Literature, specialising in Thomas Hardy, and researched dialect in Thomas Hardy's poetry for her doctoral thesis. During this research Heather recognised the necessity for students to adopt a socio-historical approach to their reading of literary texts to enable greater understanding and enjoyment of Literature. This concern supports the key quotations included in this guide to fully prepare students for the demands of the English Literature GCSE.

About the editor of this guide

Hannah Rabey is Head of English at a school in Oxfordshire. Hannah studied Literature and History at the University of East Anglia before studying for her PGCE at the University of Oxford. Hannah is a GCSE examiner and is experienced with teaching all of the texts in the 25 Key Quotations revision guide series.

Printed in Great Britain
by Amazon

78629801R00038